AFTER SILENT CENTURIES

AFTER SILENT CENTURIES

ROWAN WILLIAMS

THE PERPETUA PRESS
OXFORD

First published June 1994
Reprinted September 1994
by the Perpetua Press
26 Norham Road, Oxford OX2 6SF

ISBN 1 870882 10 5

Printed in Great Britain

CONTENTS

FOREWORD

Several of these pieces began as responses to visual works; in particular, the poems on three of the best-known and most frequently reproduced images in Eastern Christian art, the icon of Our Lady of Vladimir, probably from the twelfth century, the mosaic of Christ the ruler of all (Pantocrator) at Daphni, executed a little earlier, and the icon by Andrei Rublev showing the persons of the Trinity as angels seated at a table, from the fourteenth century. The sequence, 'Los Ninos' is prompted by Velasquez' paintings of the court dwarfs of Philip IV; from documentary sources, we know something of their histories and character. 'Kettle's Yard' alludes to a watercolour by David Jones (a friend of Jim Ede, the man whose vision established this unique 'domestic' Cambridge gallery).

The versions of poems from Welsh originals require a word of comment. The three writers represented differ widely. Ann Griffiths was a farmer's wife without formal education, who died in 1805, leaving a handful of hymns still remarkable for their bold and extravagant imagery and sustained emotional density. She wrote in conventional eighteenth century metres, with a straightforward rhyme scheme. She does not employ classical Welsh metrical forms, though she will sometimes use the alliterative idioms typical of these older forms. T. Gwynn Jones (1871-1949) was a major critical and historical writer and, in his time, an innovative poet of high reputation. Waldo Williams (1904-1971) was perhaps the foremost poet of his generation in the Welsh language, a visionary pacifist whose moral and cultural influence was (and is) immense; he was a brilliant exponent of classical Welsh forms, though he could also write in more 'free' style.

Each of these presents different problems for the translator. A close rendering of poems written in classical Welsh metre can often produce a lifeless English version, because the essential feature, the complex internal assonance and rhyming, disappears. Equally, renderings of poems in metres more recognisable to English readers, like Ann Griffiths' hymns, can soften the odd and 'baroque' quality of the strings of imagery. And to translate one of T. Gwynn Jones' less formally innovative poems in a correspondingly traditional quatrain form does him less than justice. As a result, I have adopted, for all three writers, a style of translation designed to be not at all a literal rendering, but an attempt to recreate the progressions of imagery with something of the energy they have in the original. I hope that to Welsh readers they will still be recognisable; but they are efforts to compose poems in English, rather than to give a crib to the Welsh, and I have taken considerable liberties with Ann Griffiths' verse in particular so as to present something appropriately fresh (as she deserves).

For help with these translations, I must gratefully acknowledge the kindness of my friends John Walters and Patrick Thomas. Other friends have helped with comments and reactions, over the years, to other pieces here. And I owe a great debt to Hugo Brunner and the Perpetua Press for suggesting that this collection might be worth preparing.

ROWAN WILLIAMS

DRYSTONE

In sooty streams across the hill, rough, bumpy,
contoured in jagging falls and twists, they walk
beyond the crest, beyond the muddy clough,
children's coarse pencil sentences, deep-scored,
staggering across a thick absorbing sheet, dry frontiers
on a wet land, dry streams across wet earth,
coal-dry, soot-dry, carrying the wind's black leavings
from the mill valley, but against the gales
low, subtle, huddling: needs more than wind to scatter
   them.

There is no glue, there is no mortar subtle,
solid enough for here: only the stained air blowing
up from the brewery through the lean dry gaps;
hard to know how an eye once saw the consonance,
the fit of these unsocial shapes, once saw
each one pressed to the other's frontier, every one
inside the other's edge, and conjured the dry aliens
to run, one sentence, scrawled across the sheet,
subtle against the wind, a silent spell, a plot.

SIX O'CLOCK

As the bird
rides up the sky, the last sun
looking up gilds in the hollows
of the wings, an afterthought of gift
to guests ignored and hurt, but no,
the bird rides up the sky, eyes on the night.

When the sun
levels its sights across the grass,
it packs the blades and little animals
so tight, so heavy that you wonder
why they don't tumble over
into their new, uncompromising shadow,
into their inner dark.

OUR LADY OF VLADIMIR

Climbs the child, confident,
up over breast, arm, shoulder;
while she, alarmed by his bold thrust
into her face, and the encircling hand,
looks out imploring fearfully
and, O, she cries, from her immeasurable eyes,
O how he clings, see how
he smothers every pore, like the soft
shining mistletoe to my black bark,
she says, I cannot breathe, my eyes
are aching so.

The child has overlaid us in our beds,
we cannot close our eyes,
his weight sits firmly,
fits over heart and lungs,
and choked we turn away
into the window of immeasurable dark
to shake off the insistent pushing warmth;
O how he cleaves, no peace
tonight my lady in your bower,
you, like us, restless with bruised eyes
and waking to

a shining cry on the black bark of sleep.

ADVENT CALENDAR

He will come like last leaf's fall.
One night when the November wind
has flayed the trees to bone, and earth
wakes choking on the mould,
the soft shroud's folding.

He will come like frost.
One morning when the shrinking earth
opens on mist, to find itself
arrested in the net
of alien, sword-set beauty.

He will come like dark.
One evening when the bursting red
December sun draws up the sheet
and penny-masks its eye to yield
the star-snowed fields of sky.

He will come, will come,
will come like crying in the night,
like blood, like breaking,
as the earth writhes to toss him free.
He will come like child.

RETURN JOURNEY

Why are places not neutral?
on the smoky screen of walls,
shop windows, sky and pavement spin
the flickering reels of evidence, dust crawling up
the frames, the privately detected chronicle
of clumsily arranged affairs with time and place.

Grace, yes, but damnation too dissolves
in place, so it is not the future
but the past we know to be incredible,
eluding the imagination: unmoved mover
of uncomprehending souls, shaping the mind
glued to the dusty and unwelcome screen.

Push up the blinds and in the room
nothing has gone, there in the dark
we sit unmovable, the wounds as fresh
as ever, all that was ever done
frozen against the walls in a bright moment,
iron and bitter, bright like life.

Fresh from the freezer, all the smooth pain that settled,
stayed when we went on, sat and nestled,
patiently in the corner, waiting to be collected
when we happen back, it stares in silence
at these new, would-be alien selves,
a still, unsmiling, lifelike face.

CROSSINGS

While I sit mute, suspicious of my choice
(Reserve or fluency), how do I reach
You, then, across the acres of the room?
Yes, all the platitudes are clear enough:
Muteness is eloquence, silence is the stuff
Of sharing, while hands work a busy loom;
But on your flesh my hands will still be blind.
Your face is shut. Your body gives no voice,
But charts a distance. How do we avoid
A treaty with the compromising word?
Knowing that after, when we have destroyed
The ambiguity, the precious surd
Of uncommitted quiet, we shall find
Our honesty still waits to be aligned?

You smiled, apologising for the sound —
The hollow distant penetrating hum
Of a dim underground, fathoms down from us.
In those hard channels silence yields, not here;
Under the crust, a journey's length is clear.
The traveller there has mapped his terminus,
Watches for a predicted stop to come,
Steps in the floodstream, confidently bound
A foreknown distance. I cannot select
Periods so easy from the trodden edge
Of words in flux. Prospects of an unchecked,
Unended bursting into haemorrhage
Cut me a channel where we both, pulled down
Under the hollow humming wheels, shall drown.

Tell me what I am asking, then, what plea
You hear without pronouncing. It is you
Who hold the mirror and who know the name
And will not say it; while the desperate cold
Unchristened infant, years or seconds old,
Tries its new lungs with incoherent blame,
Clench-fisted, begs the necessary clue
That holds the hand of an identity
Its lifelong distance. Absolution's cheap
This way, as I laboriously forget
The guilt of joint conspirators, asleep
Against complaining noises, bodies set
Waiting for one to learn or one to teach:
Casual midwives for miscarrying speech.

Cracks open in the floor across the years.
The rumpled bed of stone shrugs off the heat
Of wooden coverlets, impatient with the dark,
And dust no longer binds the drifting blocks.
How long before the stone has forced the locks?
How long before the flesh has split the bark?
And the foundations, naked to our feet
Carry us stumbling on a bridge that clears
The dust-choked distance? While we wait to see
A waking earth that stirs into the sun,
Our covers still are drawn, the night walks free
Between our frontiers, where no path will run.
Under the wooden shroud, under the stone,
Under the dust, the fields are locked unsown.

The shifting floor, the smeared steps inlaid,
Loosened and footprinted with journey's scars,
Is this a field for growing, this a rock
For building? no: the sedges of a marsh
Where white horizons ring the eyes, and harsh
Bird cry scratches the standing pools, to shock
The marble dark in small and passing stars;
The flats of boring exigence displayed,
Unreckoned distance. This is all I make,
A roofless acting space, a voice exposed
To drop its crying in a careless lake
Of ragged eyes, of watchers undisposed
To see or pity stale romantic scenes
Decent embarrassment clothes with safety screens.

And if I told you, should I be surprised
If you, turning your head, asked me, And why?
The choice is mine, the landscape my design,
The black my painting, and the ice my chill;
Looked bitterly at the evasive skill
That locks me up inside this private sign,
Turning a greedy fascinated eye
On an emotion still uncompromised
At its still distance. If I do not tell,
And play under the bedclothes with conceits,
What prudence keeps me in this glassy cell,
The polished atom of half-willed defeats?
Well, atoms split, my love, are lovers' death,
Out in the cold, no wind will lend us breath.

To break a lock by giving open tongue,
Stand up, come in and sing us out of doors,
I know stirs recollections in the flesh,
And blows the dust from pictures pushed away.
Collected shadows from another day —
Collected words, packed stinking, tight, unfresh,
Ready to send the shiver down old sores,
Echoes of other bodies, roundly flung
A few years' distance. And the hoarded tears,
Unheard reproaches, wait to be unlocked.
Meanwhile I thoughtfully deploy my fears,
Afraid to find my facile pities mocked,
Afraid my probing taps the blood again,
That my flesh too clouds over with the stain.

So did we ever have an assignation
Under the station clock? an intersection
Of complicated routes? Was there a break
Between connections when we might have snatched a
    word,
Unusual and hard and timely, stirred
By urgencies too close for us to make
Excuses, plead appointments for protection,
Slew our eyes round, sketch a retreat formation
Into the distance promised by the hiss
And echo of things setting to depart
All round? Eyes scattering far and anxious not to miss
Something or anything; travelling apart.
You never came, we both of us could say,
Angry, relieved, rejected, gone away.

DÉJEUNER SUR L'HERBE

Watching your hands
turn slenderly the glass
I wait for rim to snap
or bowl to spill;
but when it shall
shall there be wine to drop
on the drab summer grass
or only hours' worth of spent sands?

TWELFTH NIGHT

In the clean winter pastures of the stars
is innocence, a soft and stinging dark
bathing the cataracted eyes
of age remembering.

In the dry winter chambers of the stars
is infancy, a soul unhistoried,
breathing new air, inheriting
no dead men's speech.

Old men live long between the stars:
where else is virgin earth for minds,
for memories bursting brown skins
and spilling seed?

Old men seek sleep between the stars,
cradles between the thin white fires
to rock away the scars of choice
to a bad dream.

O if we did not know
then we should see the clean stars plain,
through the cool night, forgetting,
should come home.

O if we did not see
then we should know the empty air,
the fields of sleep, the fresh and unimagined
scents of spilled grass or leaf.

Now when the stars have called to welcome us,
how shall we not run home?
the far side of the desert promises
tearless childhood,

Now that the stars speak clear to us
the language of our marketplace, and cry
come buy, you poor, for innocence
is cheap tonight.

Journeys for old men are not kind
when comfort's sold to buy the single pearl;
yet the child's eye is lifetime's worth of gold,
world's worth of pilgrimage.

Journeys for old men are not mapped,
but for the backward lodestone of desire
for that oasis where the mind is quenched
under still leaves.

Once in the house we saw the trap:
their eyes told all, the childish mother
nursing the knowing mortal child,
a mocking boy.

Once in the house, the stars smiled back
pleased and sardonic at their wit;
sweet-baited lines that catch unpityingly
in the soft places.

Behind the stars no holiday,
no taking out of recollection, but
a cup pressed full of pasts
incalculable.

Behind the stars no happy end,
no dissolution of our scars,
no garden plot, no spilling grass:
the cot is empty.

Where has the child gone, to what fire,
what rubbish bin, what coins were laid
to close his eyes? give us at least
the choice of sending flowers.

Where has the child gone? is the watched sky
a single cenotaph for dead simplicity,
the stars a moss-grown requiescat
in half-remembered alphabets?

And we, conscripted mourners for the funeral,
hands full of soil, left sleepless
with the small corpse, until grey dawn
summons us out?

And we, the prisoners of a narrative
of deaths and soiling, heavy as the world,
of stale and endless air, of age,
scents of senility?

The child says, True, this market does not sell
forgetfulness. In a still pool
I hold a glass to all your storms,
to all your eyes.

The child says, True, for nothing is undone
beyond the stars, the tree that grows tonight
is hung with all the lives of men and women,
all your deaths.

You still are children, innocence not gone,
what memory of yours is worth the name?
where were you when the world's foundations
set in children's blood?

You still are children; all that you have known
is fear, not guilt, have felt the blade,
but not the handle of the moulder's knife
carving a mind.

Your histories belong to me; here is
not innocence but absolution, for
your scars are true, but I (always)
will bleed in them.

Your memories belong to me; I lie
awake at night and see for ever, while
the stars shall fall like leaves
to cover you.

GREAT SABBATH

Unwatched, the seventh dawn spreads,
Light smoothing out the sky, firm hands
Smearing a damp clay horizon-wide.
They wake, then lie unsurely side by side,
Knowing the ache and pull of novel bands,
The night's new memories grinding in their heads,

Not understood, their bodies newly strange.
Outside, the new light soaks the ground;
They chill, turn in towards each other's heat,
Then roll apart to test uncertain feet
On unknown earth. The dripping dawn around
Confirms the unformed fear. The world can change.

Outside an absence. While they learned and slept,
It had drawn off behind the sky's stone face.
The world between their bodies and their palms
Is left to turn. The silence calms.
The morning's news is plain; the centre space
Is empty. Under the trees where he once stepped

It is for you to go. Under the gaping sky
You wake, he sleeps, you make, he lies at rest.
He will not come again; last night you made
A future he will not invade.
Today the sun is buried, unexpressed;
You shall shape how to live and how to die.

You shall make change. He leaves no room
For his own hand; you shall be history,
You shall build heaven, you shall quarry hell.
No one shall say you have (or not) made well.

And, bored and pious, talk of mystery,
When weeds are choking up his tomb.

We make, he sleeps. Only his bloody dreams
Tell him the works of freedom on the earth.
Your liberty his flight, your future and his death.
He dreams your hell for you to draw your breath,
Out of his emptiness he lets your birth,
It is his silence echoes back the screams.

For they have not forgotten everything;
They wake and lie unsurely side by side
And listen to a laboured, steady breath,
Insistent, unconsoled, remembered death.
A small-hours passing on the turning tide,
Alone and never taught what key to sing.

He will not come again, not in the form
He walked on your first earth. But will you know
Him when he slips, a dosser, through the door?
Oh yes. Who else will touch the raw
Salt, unhealed memory of worlds ago,
Whispering, once you knew, once you were warm.

Listen for promises, fantasize for care,
And you will fill the neutral sky with lead,
Make chains to stop the quiet flow of chance,
Sell all your working for a stripper's dance.
He chose his death; why can he not be dead,
And leave the bloody dreams at home elsewhere?

Drink up your tears; you can no longer need
The luxury of an old, cheap compassion.
To bury him may be a heavy cost,
But buys our future when today is lost,

Buys the clean stone from which we can refashion
Our image scarred by his remembered greed.

He asks his present back; the clay-daubed hands
Are picking at the dyke. Weep and you will unmix
The mortar, and the salt black sea will run
And catch and trip and down us, one by one.
For walls are weaker than their strongest bricks.
Behind the stone, the moon-fed tide expands

To flood our fens. We walk with desperate care,
The locks are fragile and the wind is swelling,
Windows will rattle us awake, eyes wide,
To stare, lying unsurely side by side,
Quiet and fearful; there is no telling
What dreams will flesh out of the noisy air.

The stones had fallen down. We woke too late.
He has unlatched the house, smashed through the pains,
While we slept out our sixth and darkest night,
And taken back his gross seigneurial right.
Today he swills the cultivated plains,
Salting our clay; reclaiming our estate.

OYSTERMOUTH CEMETERY

Grass laps; the stone keels jar,
scratch quietly in the rippling soil.
The little lettered masts dip slowly
in a little breeze, the anchors here
are very deep among the shells.

Not till the gusty day
when a last angel tramples down
into the mud his dry foot hissing,
down to the clogged forgotten shingle,
till the bay boils and shakes,

Not till that day shall the cords snap
and all the little craft float stray
on unfamiliar tides, to lay their freight
on new warm shores, on those strange islands
where their tropic Easter landfall is.

THIRD STATION

Fall. And between the grey air
and your stone back will run the stream,
quick, cold, of weeping breath,
the mind's sour spit of overnight,
coating the broken skin against its load.

Lift. And between the stone spine
and the sun's weight are caught
the leavings of the mind, the grounds
that cloud the bottom of the heart, and shaken
bitter it. Press to the sun your skin.

Turn. And between the weights of heaven and self
rub small the crying grain and burst
the puckered gelid streams. Wind tight the press
and mill our parching salt, our black and needful flour.
Bread. Tears.

BEREAVEMENTS

In memory of Jim and Letty Morgan

Beginning with the purchase order:
Notice was served on some years' livelihood
(no choice: lucid imperatives drive rapidly;
they need their motorways), and then
the hospital, and notice served on some years' love ·
(or something like it), confident highspeed
mortality (no choice, not even purchase)
So that he watched the dusty rubbled bed,
those months, the engines ploughing up
                                some years of him,
the furrows slowly merging in the flesh and mud,
the shrinking face, the swelling pools, bewildered,
waiting for clearance. Till the knot was tied,
black gravel rollered down, where the imperatives
run smoothly off for the horizon. In the house,
behind the window she put in out back, he sits
and sees remembered grass still springing underneath
the lucid wheels. He will not go,
not leave the stranded house; his livelihood,
his years, are razored down to this,
                              eyes at this window.
Nowhere else; no choice.

PANTOCRATOR: DAPHNI

Pillars of dusty air beneath the dome
of golden leaden sky strain to bear up
his sweaty heaviness, his bulging eyes
drawn inwards to their private pain,
his hands arthritic with those inner knots,
his blessings set aside.
He has forgotten us, this one,
and sees a black unvisitable place
where from all ages to all ages he will die
and cry, creating in his blood
congealing galaxies of heat and weight.
Why should he bless or need an open book?
we know the words as well as he,
the names, Alpha, Omega,
fire from fire, we know your cry
out of the dusty golden whirlwind, how you forget
us so that we can be.

AUGUSTINE

Take off your shoes,
paddle again in the hot dust.
My mother baked me on these hot stones,
a foreign father handled, pressed
and broke and packed me back
to feed his furnaces
here on the baking dust.

Take down the curtains
round your hot bed.
The long moon shines away
back through the talking hours
of young men's faces damp with eloquence.
The midnight dust under the window
paints me my shadow, light and cold.

Take it and read.
Not now the child's lost voice
climbing the garden wall
in that exact and northern afternoon
to coax me into play. Take up
your shadow, read me
from the bakestone squares.

Take up the stones
and find the choked foundations.
My fingers push the dust away
from broken, staring faces,
half my heart. The world's mosaic
shattered for centuries in the sand
before my memory.

Take up your voice
and tell your shadow's story. If
I weave this web out of my belly,
spread it between the broken ribs
of the hot square, then shall I catch
the winged and stinging visitor,
breaker of each night's sleep?

Take off your shoes.
This dust is mine, this knotted web
is mine, this shadow
is my shape for you, and when
the hot dust scalds your eyes to tears,
who is it weeps with you to soak
your dust to speaking clay?

INDOORS

Beaten and close the earth in here,
small blunt old fingers day to day
packing the corners, moulding down serrated
    tops
along the walls; then pull and plait the springing
    brambles
into screens and springing grills, a scrollworked
    coverlet,
Sometimes the spines will catch, lift up a flake of
    settled skin,
sometimes a drop swells of small thin old blood.
    Or earth
runs in the cleft of a white hard old scar, mind
    wanders to
the recollected blow and bleeding, for an hour or
    two, from day to day,
whispering, familiar.

This is the house that years built, dropping soil
from the loose screes. Straddling the hill, the
    cottage sheds its tiles,
the books begin to corrugate with damp. Home
is the cleft where earth runs, and a little old thin
    blood,
home's where the hurt is, white and familiar as a
    bone.

RUBLEV

One day, God walked in, pale from the grey steppe,
slit-eyed against the wind, and stopped,
said, Colour me, breathe your blood into my mouth.

I said, Here is the blood of all our people,
these are their bruises, blue and purple,
gold, brown, and pale green wash of death.

These (god) are the chromatic pains of flesh,
I said, I trust I make you blush,
O I shall stain you with the scars of birth

For ever. I shall root you in the wood,
under the sun shall bake you bread
of beechmast, never let you forth

To the white desert, to the starving sand.
But we shall sit and speak around
one table, share one food, one earth.

SNOW FEN

On these drum-tight pegged flats, it does not fall
in blankets rucked around the soil,
soft fleece around the raw veins, no,
but drains away the colourblocks
leaving the pool of hollow bone.
It has called back the bleach, the chalk,
the pulse along a whistling buried wire
below the marsh, the monody,
bat-pitched, of the electric stars.

Sketches of street and hedge
and scribbled farms, the pencilled query notes
against the ledger, smear down steadily
to a grey page, rinsed at last
to its sharp grain again;
an unsuccessful cold and clichéd snap
soaks out, the canvas is tacked down
drum-tight and thirsty for the brush
of some less academic sky.

KETTLE'S YARD
4 MARCH 1984

Pebbles and sea-light,
drift of grain across an ebbing floor,
land's end. The wind is sharp as gulls
past David's Pembroke window,
lettering the stars across
a winter wall.

The gods are grey
and concave, finger-printed into hollow eyes,
their stones warm ash. Fires on the shore
fold when the night drops and we build
the ferns to pack us warm
in crackling beds.

A bell for morning,
pebbles at dawn push damp and black,
teasing awake. The wind is sharp as gulls,
so up the stairs: the sand swells round
a blunted skull. I wash
my face in stone.

SEPTEMBER BIRDS

Down in the small hollow where the currents shift
slowly, and drop with the thinning sun, the crows
float, crowding the shallow slopes of air,
and vague as specks of stubble fire: the sun
has scattered them from thinning flames, has clapped
a hollow hand, once, twice, a glowing wooden gong,
a log that cracks sharp in the ashes, and
has given wings to the charred dust.
                                    Later, it hangs
moonlike and old with woodsmoke in a black tree
up on the ridge. The crows, snared by the netted oaks,
stick still, the scraps of paper from the fire, yesterday's
    news
and last week's envelopes. The words come back on
    them
at sunrise, faintly traced. Sometimes we read
our home addresses.

THE WHITE HORSE

They guessed, as they dug off the turf,
the sign that waited for them
where the chalk lines fell out,
scattered and compact,
bones for an augury, divining stalks,
the cupped hill's ideogram: *Beast*, it said,
but do not be afraid.
This is no foreign word:
under the swell of dredging labour
it is quick and clear;
the white earth runs like water.

CORNISH WATERS

Above Boscastle

Grey, warm and stony air
hangs from the clouds in swaying pillars,
and the rain, complex, occasional,
pricks a soft skin.

The green slopes heave
down through the cloud, against the sand,
swallowed and drained off at the bay,
collapsed at journey's end.

Up on the stormy hills
the travellers drop through the grey troughs,
their breath filled up with rain,
eyes under water.

And from the sea,
the level concrete of the sea, who looks,
unmoved and private on the quay
at the land's wrecks?

St Endellion: in church

Between the twinkling granite spars,
the tide is almost at the roof,
pushing the jostling drift of beams.

Lapping insistent words in flood
cajole and smooth Atlantic scarps;
the rock grows deep around the swell.

The little waves will clap their hands,
after the rhythm drops; the stains
paint little transient peaks of dark.

Blackness of words, dense symphonies,
push at the jostling drift of beams
that seal and smooth the granite well.

Dead wood, the drift of nameless craft,
light with the memories of drowning,
hedges the fields of rhythmic dark.

The tide is turning with the roof still dry.

Goonhilly Downs

Wrapped in damp furs, the cold Sidonians
looked in the pits of tin and bought
and hammered out a tongue for awkward contracts,
laying the spiky consonants of Canaan
around the mines, the dangerous dark pools,
where wealth and death, with their loud vowels, hide.

Wedges of thorn, the spiky bone expecting
flesh that will never come, drop a black image
on to the moor's puddles, where the sky,
plain between showers, shines, a thin and equal light;
and in the mirror, the Phoenician consonants
tread back into their distant native text:

Lands before commerce, loss, desire
voiced on the thorn complaints and bargaining;
before the showers come back to dig the moor
with metal hollows mined down to the vein.
A, says the wind, and, when the first rain falls,
O, says the scarred pool round its fractured spines.

Camelford (in honour of Regional Water Companies)

Rain is transparent, irresistible,
extravagant and obstinate,
it never will be wooed, to come or go,
like words, or grace.

Rain can be caught, drunk, trapped,
woven with particles of solid dark,
thickened in renal channels, flavoured
with compromising flesh.

Rain must be purchased in a thirsty time
(when knots of charity are dry to breaking point),
clouded and dense with lodging in the guts
of canny men.

Rain sours in the ruts of foresight, payment
salts it to piss, so that it cannot fall
cold on a breaking skin, graceful
for tongue and stomach.

Rain's not exhausted, can't be wooed to go;
the dark still gathers out of which,
heavy and wet as words or grace, it falls
to wash sores; flood banks.

BACH FOR THE CELLO

By mathematics we shall come to heaven.
This page the door of God's academy
for the geometer,

Where the pale lines involve a continent,
transcribe the countryside of formal light,
kindle with friction.

Passion will scorch deep in these sharp canals:
under the level moon, desire runs fast,
the flesh aches on its string,
without consummation,

Without loss.

LOS NINOS

Nino de Vallecas

Look. Big feet and chubby legs
stretched out.
Again. The mouth, lifting a little,
knowingly. I am unhappy; I have noticed
that this is not an accident.
Again. The eyes reach vaguely.
I am unhappy. What will you do?
Are you my friend? What will you give
a child disguised
as a man dressed as a child?

Don Sebastian

What you must do is look me in the eyes
today, the eyes I turned on them, King Philip,
the Infantes, the Inquisitor, the Cardinal my master,
saying, Now, laugh; pity; befriend,
if you so dare. They looked across my head,
friendly and sorry; my ears were close enough
to hear their heaving stomachs' mirth.
So here I sit, stranger, at your eyes for once,
not at your reeking crotch. Now:
pity; befriend. I do not think
I shall be first to drop my gaze, and you may guess
what these cold knuckles hold so close.

Don Pedro

I am the little man
that potent fellows fear
for I run chuckling

42

between their legs,
stealing the privilege
of your stuffed trunks.

Down where you do not come
there lives the world of little folk,
bright, bitter, sniggering
at your swelled dramas. Why?
down here we're hungry:
concentrates the mind.

HYMN FOR THE MERCY SEAT

Wonder is what the angels' eyes hold, wonder:
The eyes of faith, too, unbelieving in the strangeness,
Looking on him who makes all being gift,
Whose overflowing holds, sustains,
Who sets what is in shape,
Here in the cradle, swaddled, homeless,
And here adored by the bright eyes of angels,
The great Lord recognised.

Sinai ablaze, the black pall rising,
Through it the horn's pitch, high, intolerable,
And I, I step across the mortal frontier
Into the feast, safe in my Christ from slaughter.
Beyond that boundary all loss is mended,
The wilderness is filled, for he,
Broker between the litigants, stands in the breach,
Offers himself for peace.

Between the butchered thieves, the mercy seat, the healing,
The place for him to test death's costs,
Who powers his very killers' arms,
Drives in the nails that hold him, while he pays
The debt of brands torn from the bonfire,
Dues to his Father's law, the flames of justice
Bright for forgiveness now, administering
Liberty's contract.

Soul, look. This is the place where all kings' monarch
Rested a corpse, the maker of our rest, and in
His stillness all things always move,
Within his buried silence.
Song for the lost, and life; wonder
For angels' straining eyes, God's flesh.
They praise together, they adore,
'To him', they shout, 'only to him'.

And I, while there is breath left to me,
Say, Thanksgiving, with a hundred thousand words,
Thanksgiving: that there is a God to worship,
There is an everlasting matter for my singing;
Who with the worst of us, in what
He shares with me, cried under tempting,
A child and powerless, the boundless
Living true God.

Flesh rots: instead, aflame, along with heaven's singers,
I shall pierce through the veil, into the land
Of infinite astonishment, the land
Of what was done at Calvary;
I shall look on what never can be seen, and still
Shall live, look on the one who died and who still lives
And shall; look in eternal jointure and communion,
Not to be parted.

I shall lift up the name that God
Sets out to be a mercy seat, a healing, and the veils,
And the imaginings and shrouds have gone, because
My soul stands now, his finished likeness,
Admitted now to share his secret, that his blood and hurt
Showed once, now I shall kiss the Son
And never turn away again. And never
Turn away.

From the Welsh of Ann Griffiths

I SAW HIM STANDING

Under the dark trees, there he stands,
there he stands; shall he not draw my eyes?
I thought I knew a little
how he compels, beyond all things, but now
he stands there in the shadows. It will be
Oh, such a daybreak, such bright morning,
when I shall wake to see him
as he is.

He is called Rose of Sharon, for his skin
is clear, his skin is flushed with blood,
his body lovely and exact; how he compels
beyond ten thousand rivals. There he stands,
my friend, the friend of guilt and helplessness,
to steer my hollow body
over the sea.

The earth is full of masks and fetishes,
what is there here for me? are these like him?
Keep company with him and you will know:
no kin, no likeness to those empty eyes.
He is a stranger to them all, great Jesus.
What is there here for me? I know
what I have longed for. Him to hold
me always.

From the Welsh of Ann Griffiths

46

STRATA FLORIDA

Wind murmurs in the trees at Ystrad Fflur
but does not wake
the dozen abbots dozing in their tombs
while the leaves shake.

Dead with his clever verses, Dafydd too
lies in his bed
Among forgotten warlords, swords dulled,
armour shed.

Summer will come and rouse the wind-stripped trees.
But not the men.
Stones unobtrusively decay. They will not
stand again.

Defeat, oblivion, rotting monuments
of dead belief.
Why is it then I find no words, here, quietly,
for private grief?

From the Welsh of T. Gwynn Jones

SONG FOR A BOMB

I split and scatter him who splits and scatters,
And in my falling there is Adam's Fall.
Where in this vacuum will you find purpose,
Where is the pattern where a purpose dwells?

It only takes the naked brain to think me,
It only takes a human hand to shape,
And youthful nimbleness to bring to action.
What are you waiting for? Create.

My master quietly pursues his business,
Patient untying of the knotted heart.
Till, fearfully and wonderfully crafted,
Last of his servants, forth I come to wait.

My master is the worm that gnaws the root,
My master is the canker in the tree.
But I shall tidy him away for ever
On to the bonfire of death's ecstasy.

From the Welsh of Waldo Williams

IN THE DAYS OF CAESAR

In the days of Caesar, when his subjects went to be
    reckoned,
there was a poem made, too dark for him (naive with
    power) to read.
It was a bunch of shepherds who discovered
in Bethlehem of Judah, the great music beyond reason
    and reckoning:
shepherds, the sort of folk who leave the ninety-nine
    behind
so as to bring the stray back home, they heard it clear,
the subtle assonances of the day, dawning toward cock-
    crow,
the birthday of the Lamb of God, shepherd of mortals.

Well, little people, and my little nation, can you see
the secret buried in you, that no Caesar ever captures in
    his lists?
Will not the shepherd come to fetch us in our desert,
gathering us in to give us birth again, weaving us into
    one
in a song heard in the sky over Bethlehem?
He seeks us out as wordhoard for his workmanship, the
    laureate of heaven.

From the Welsh of Waldo Williams

AFTER SILENT CENTURIES

For the Catholic martyrs of Wales

The centuries of silence gone, now let me weave a
    celebration;
Because the heart of faith is one, the moment glows in
    which
Souls recognise each other, one with the great tree's
    kernel at the root of things.

They are at one with the light, where peace masses
    and gathers
In the infinities above my head; and, where the sky
    moves into night,
Then each one is a spyhole for my darkened eyes,
    lifting the veil.

John Roberts, Trawsfynydd: a pauper's priest,
Breaking bread for the journey when the plague
    weighed on them,
Knowing the power of darkness on its way to break,
    crumble, his flesh.

John Owen, carpenter: so many hiding places
Made by his tireless hands for old communion's sake,
So that the joists are not undone, the beam pulled
    from the roof.

Richard Gwyn: smiling at what he saw in their faces,
    said,
'I've only sixpence for your fine' — pleading his
    Master's case,
His charges (for his life) were cheap as that.

50

Oh, they ran swift and light. How can we weigh
  them, measure them,
The muster of their troops, looking down into
  damnation?
Nothing, I know, can scatter those bound by the
  paying of one price,

The final, silent tariff. World given in exchange for
  world,
The far frontiers of agony to buy the Spirit's
  leadership,
The flower paid over for the root, the dying grain to
  be his cradle.

Their guts wrenched out after the trip to torment on
  the hurdle,
And before the last gasp when the ladder stood in
  front of them
For the soul to mount, up to the wide tomorrow of
  their dear Lord's Golgotha.

You'd have a tale to tell of them, a great, a memorable
  tale,
If only, Welshmen, you were, after all, a people.

From the Welsh of Waldo Williams

DIE BIBELFORSCHER

For the Protestant martyrs of the Third Reich

Earth is a hard text to read; but the king
has put his message in our hands, for us to carry
sweating, whether the trumpets of his court
sound near or far. So for these men:
they were the bearers of the royal writ,
clinging to it through spite and hurts and wounding.

The earth's round fullness is not like a parable, where
    meaning
breaks through, a flash of lightning, in the humid, heavy
    dusk;
imagination will not conjure into flesh the depths
of fire and crystal sealed under castle walls of wax, but
    still
they kept their witness pure in Buchenwald,
pure in the crucible of hate penning them in.

They closed their eyes to doors that might have opened
if they had put their names to words of cowardice;
they took their stand, backs to the blank wall, face to face
    with savagery,
and died there, with their filth and piss flowing together,
arriving at the gates of heaven,
their fists still clenched on what the king had written.

Earth is a hard text to read. But what we can be certain of
is that the screaming mob is insubstantial mist;
in the clear sky, the thundering assertions fade to nothing.
There the Lamb's song is sung, and what it celebrates
is the apocalypse of a glory
pain lays bare.

From the Welsh of Waldo Williams